CONTENTS

WET

The adventures of a water drop

It was raining. Amy stood on the pavement looking at a puddle. As she watched, a big drop of water splashed into the puddle. 'Where will it go?' she wondered.

CHANNEL TUNNEL

1 People first thought of digging a tunnel between England and France in 1802, but the work will not be finished until 1994.

2 The Channel Tunnel is 49 km long and is 40 m under the sea bed. There are three tunnels, two for trains and a service tunnel in the middle.

3 Eleven huge digging machines were needed to build it.

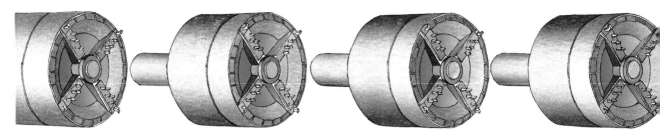

4 The rock under the English Channel is **sedimentary**. It is made of different layers that have settled and gone solid over thousands of years, like this:

A layer of clay was made from bits of silt from rivers that settled and were pressed down by the next layer.

A layer of sandstone made from sand particles.

A layer of limestone made from bits of dead sea creatures.

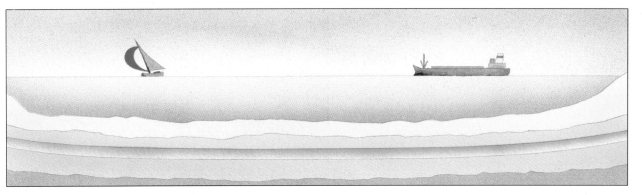

5 The tunnel was dug through a layer of chalk marl, which is a mixture of chalk and clay. This is good rock for tunnelling because it is quite soft and water cannot pass through it.

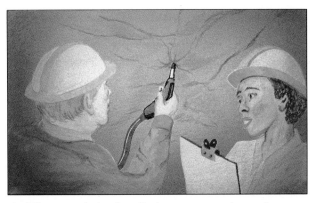

6 The rock isn't all the same, though. Geologists had to check it before cutting it, using special probe drills. You don't want a sudden surprise half way across the Channel!

7 While they were checking, they found fossils of Arctic plants, snails and beetles from just after the last Ice Age.

8 On 1st December 1990 the first of the three tunnels met in the middle. The people working the digging machines were 40m under the sea bed and about 25 km away from either end of the tunnel.

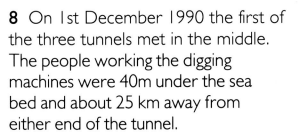

What sort of problems do you think they had when they were digging the tunnel?

The first two people to meet between France and England without leaving dry land.

LANDFORMS

Wow!

The Grand Canyon is over a mile deep!

How frightened the first settlers in Northern Ireland must have been when they saw the Giant's Causeway! Who could have carved these huge rocky columns?

We now know that these rocks were not made by giants. They formed millions of years ago when there were **volcanoes** in Ireland. They were once part of a huge river of **lava** that flowed into the sea. The cold sea water made the lava harden and crack to form these tall perfectly shaped columns of rock.

This is the Grand Canyon, in the southern United States. It was dug by the waters of the Colorado River. As the water flows through this channel it carries away tiny amounts rock and sand. Slowly, over millions of years, it has worn through many layers rock. Now you can hardly see the river at the bottom of the canyon.

Lulworth Cove in Dorset

This is what can happen to rock when one piece of the Earth's crust pushes on another. You can see that the layers of rock have folded.

Movements in the Earth's crust are usually so slow we can't feel them, but sometimes it happens very suddenly, causing an earthquake. This damage was caused by an earthquake in southern Italy. (You can read about the Earth's crust on page 9.)

OLD AS THE HILLS

When people think something is very old they sometimes say 'as old as the hills' – but how old is a hill? The hills that make up the Scottish Highlands are 500 million years old. The highest point is 1342 metres.

The Himalayan mountain range to the north of India began to appear about 20 million years ago, and it is still getting higher. The highest point is 8856 metres!

Mount Fuji in Japan is a **volcano**. According to a Japanese legend, it began to grow in the year 286 BC, during an earthquake. Like all volcanoes, it is formed from melted rock that erupts from deep underground.

crust

core

mantle

If the earth were the size of an egg, the crust would be as thin as the shell.

INDIA

Wow! The north of Scotland used to be next to a bit of Canada. Now they are 4800 km apart.

The Earth seems very solid, but the cold hard stuff we walk on is a crust less than 50 kilometres deep. This is very thin compared with the size of the Earth. Underneath the crust, the rock is so red hot that it is soft.

The Earth's crust is not one solid sheet. It is cracked into separate pieces and each piece is moving very slowly, less than a centimetre a year, floating on the liquid rock underneath.

This movement causes earthquakes and volcanoes as pieces of crust separate, collide, or slide against one another. The Himalayas are forming because the piece of crust that makes up India is moving north, crashing into Asia and causing the crust to fold and push upwards.

This is just what happened to the British hills – but they formed so much longer ago that they have been worn down again!

TOIL OR SOIL

Plants can be grown without soil. You may have **germinated** a bean or pea seed in a jar with some tissue paper.

MY STRAWBERRIES WILL BE READY TO PICK ON THE 29th OF JUNE

The plants in this greenhouse are also growing without soil. Special gravel is used instead of soil and water. Water is made to flow through the gravel at a rate which gives the plants just the right amount of moisture. A special mixture of chemicals is added to the water and this gives the plants exactly the **nutrients** they need.

It seems very clever to be able to grow plants without soil, but it does take a lot of work. People do it because they can control the growing conditions exactly to make sure that the crop is good quality and ready on time.

Growing plants in soil is a lot easier because the soil does the work. No one has to make sure the flowers in this meadow are watered. When it rains the water soaks down into the soil. No one has to give them a special mixture of chemicals to make sure they have the nutrients they need to grow. They are growing in soil which contains what they need.

The nutrients are there because soil is the home of many creatures. Some of them are so tiny they can only be seen with a microscope. Dead leaves and other plant and animal waste are broken down by these creatures and the nutrients inside them can be used by new growing plants. They take them in through the roots.

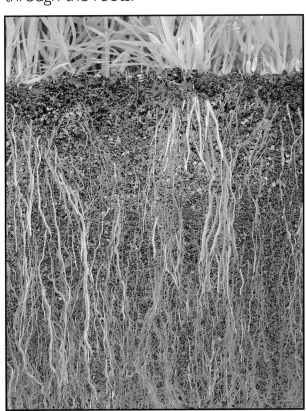

Sometimes we add fertilizers to the soil to give plants even more nutrients. But even if we add fertilizers, we can't control the conditions exactly.

MOUNT PINATUBO

I live in the Philippines, in the Pacific Ocean. There are over 200 **volcanoes** here, and I live in a town called Castillejos which is near a volcano called Mount Pinatubo.

Mount Pinatubo hadn't erupted since 1380. That's more than 600 years ago. We didn't think it would ever erupt again, but on 9th June 1991 it did. A silent column of ash, steam, and red hot rocks shot 24 kilometres into the atmosphere in three minutes, brushing the clouds away. My parents were terrified that we would all be killed.

The sky was dark. Our whole village was covered in grey ash – where there had been green fields and crops there was now just greyness. When my parents saw this they were very sad because all their crops were ruined.

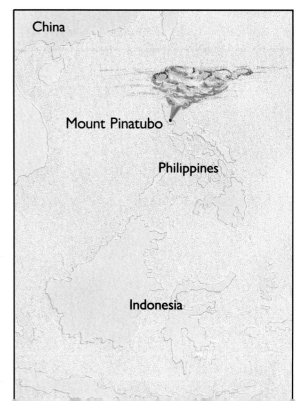

China

Mount Pinatubo

Philippines

Indonesia

It was strange living in a one-colour world. At first I thought it was fun, because it was all so new and different, and my brothers, sisters, friends and I didn't think of the danger. Then all the ash in the air began to hurt our eyes and throats and we started to cough a lot. It wasn't fun after all.

My parents said we would have to leave our village. It was raining a lot, and the rivers had filled up with banks of mud which could bury us.

Now I am living in an evacuation camp with my family and the other people from my village. We live in a very small tent. Our water comes from a huge tank, and we are given food by international aid organizations.

We can still see our mountain from the camp. We feel safer here, but it would be nice to go home.

LIFE IN A ROTTEN NEIGHBOURHOOD

Soil is much more than just tiny pieces of rock – it's a whole neighbourhood. Thousands of different kinds of living things live in or on soil and as they do, they help to make the soil.

Sand

Soil

When plants die or lose their leaves, the dead plant material rots and becomes part of the soil.

Fungi get their food by making dead plants and animals rot.

The droppings from animals also become part of the soil.

Earthworms live on the material rotting in the soil. They swallow soil at their head end, **digest** some of the material it contains and then push the soil out at their tail end. They improve soil by mixing it up, getting air into it and speeding up rotting.

Earthworm

Soil in different places

The kinds of creatures that live on soil and how active they are can change the way soil looks.

The soil in most British woodlands contains a lot of rotting material. This makes the soil look dark brown or black.

In the tropical rainforests the soil contains very little rotting material. Any plant remains which fall to the ground are rapidly broken down and used again, so there is not much there at any one time.

Forests in countries where it is much colder than Britain usually have a thin layer of rotting material at the surface and a thicker layer of soil underneath. The layers do not get mixed because earthworms can't live in this cold soil.

MINERALS

Mineral is one of those words that seems to have lots of different meanings. One of the reasons for this is that there are so many different minerals – several thousand of them.

Milk has minerals for strong bones and teeth.

Canada is a we. country because has lots . minera

I only drink mineral water nowadays.

Rocks are made of minerals and most rocks are a mix of several different kinds of minerals. If you look at some rocks closely you can make out the different minerals they contain.

This boy is looking at an emerald

Some minerals like emeralds and rubies are valuable because they are rare and beautiful. People mine them from deep underground.

Many minerals dissolve in water. Water that contains a lot of dissolved minerals is often called mineral water.

You need to eat minerals in order to grow and stay healthy. Your teeth and bones are hard because of the minerals they contain.

Vegetable oil is made from vegetables

but mineral oil comes from oil wells.

SIR GALE FORCE

Hero of the battle against the Armada

In July 1588, Queen Elizabeth I must have wondered how much longer she would be Queen of England. King Philip of Spain had ordered the mighty Spanish Armada to attack England. It didn't seem possible that Sir Francis Drake and the English navy would be able to fight off the fleet of 120 warships that were sailing toward her coast – but they did.

Weather scientists have studied reports of the weather conditions at the time of the Spanish attack. They think that the Armada was really defeated by the English weather.

Remember that in those days, ships had no engines. They were sailing ships and the speed and direction of the wind made a big difference to how fast they could travel, how well they could fight and whether or not they would make it home safely.

The destruction of the Armada began on 7th August when the Spanish fleet was anchored off France. The wind was blowing from the south west, away from the English fleet and toward the Spanish. (It often blows this way.) That night, when the **tide** also began to flow toward the Spanish boats the English were able to use a cunning tactic.

They set light to eight of their ships and set them floating toward the Spanish. The burning ships had no sailors on board. The wind and tide simply pushed them along. The Spanish sailors had to get out of the way of the burning ships as best they could in the dark. By morning, the great fleet was completely disorganized.

That was when the English ships attacked. The direction of the wind made it easy for them to bear down on the Spanish. The Armada was trapped between the English navy and the French coast. As they tried to escape, the wind kept pushing them toward the sandbanks off the coast of Holland where they could easily run aground. The English won the battle and sank several of the largest ships of the Armada.

The following day, the wind kept the Spanish trapped against the Dutch sandbanks. The English couldn't keep up the fight because they were running short of ammunition but the Spanish didn't know this. When the wind changed direction and allowed the Armada to escape, they decided to sail northward rather than face another battle. They planned to get home by sailing right around Britain.

A week later, there was a terrible storm. The English ships which were chasing the Armada were able to shelter in port but the Spanish just had to cope as best they could. By 21st September, the remains of the Armada that had made it around Scotland was off the west coast of Ireland. Then an even worse storm struck and at least 17 ships sank.

Attacking England destroyed the mighty Spanish Armada in 1588 but does the English navy deserve all the credit? The story would have had a very different ending if the Spanish had been lucky enough to have the weather on their side.

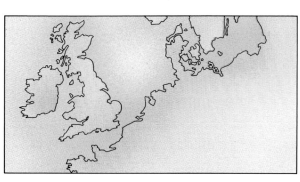

You could trace the route of the battle on a map of Northern Europe.

WEATHER WOMAN

Eleanor Crompton is a forecaster working at the Cardiff Weather Centre. She prepares weather forecasts for the local radio stations and gives more detailed advice to farmers, sailors, aeroplane pilots and other people who have a special interest in knowing what the weather in the area will be like.

Eleanor gives the weather forecast for Cardiff

The sun shines in Cardiff

Storm over South Wales

'To forecast how weather will change, you have to know what it is like at the moment. An important part of our work is taking measurements and observing the weather here in South Wales.

'People all over the world are collecting similar information about the weather in their area and more data comes in from ships, aeroplanes, weather balloons and satellites. The information is shared with all forecasters through a telecommunications network.

Waves hit Welsh coast

'Weather is all about air. We have to know what the air is like. What temperature is the air? How damp is it? Is the dampness falling, like rain or snow or is it in the form of mist, clouds or invisible water **vapour**? What are the clouds like and where are they in the sky?

'We also need to know what the air is doing. Which direction is it moving in and how fast? Air moves up and down as well as sideways and the air several kilometres above our heads affects our weather too.

Weather balloon

Flooding in Wales

Eleanor studies a weather chart

'Very powerful computers sort out all this data and produce maps showing what the weather is like over a large area. The computer updates this information every few hours. It has also been programmed to make predictions about where the air will move and how it will behave over the next few days. We use this information to make a forecast of what sort of weather the air will bring.'

IS THE WORLD'S CLIMATE CHANGING?

In recent years, unusual or unexpected weather conditions have brought suffering to millions of people in many countries, including Britain.

Recording the weather in Botswana

To see if this unusual weather is part of a change in the Earth's **climate**, weather scientists from all over the world are making records of the weather in their area and comparing it with records made in the past. This record was made at Kew, near London, in December 1886.

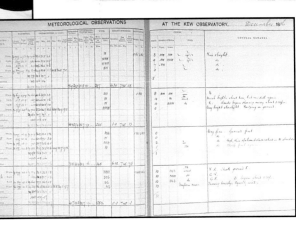

Unusual weather conditions are very often recorded by people who aren't weather scientists. This picture, painted in 1683, shows London during a winter so cold that the River Thames froze over.

Can you think of some ways of recording the weather?

To look further back in time, scientists examine the places where nature has recorded the weather. Every tree grows a new ring around its trunk each year. If the weather is good with plenty of rain, the rings are wider apart.

This scientist is cutting through some ice drilled up in Antarctica. The scientist can tell from studying this what the weather was like there in the past.

Most scientists believe that the Earth's climate is changing, and has been changing ever since the Earth began. The worry is that the damage and changes that we are causing to the Earth through pollution and the destruction of the rainforests might be causing our climate to change much more rapidly than ever before. This picture shows a rainforest which has been cut down in Malaysia.

GLOSSARY

Climate
The climate of a place is the weather conditions usually found there, including the seasonal changes that happen during the year.

Digest
Foods have to be broken down into simpler substances in a special way to turn them into a form that a living body can use. This special way is called digestion. Your food starts to be digested as soon as you start to chew it.

Germinate
When a seed germinates, a shoot and a root sprout from it and start to grow.

Lava
Lava is the melted rock that is thrown out of a volcano. It hardens as it cools.

Mineral
Minerals are one of the substances that make up a rock. There are lots of different kinds of mineral. Some are coloured, others are clear and transparent like glass. Some are very hard indeed, others are so soft you can scratch them with your fingernail.

Nutrients
Nutrients are the substances that an animal or a plant needs to have if it is going to stay healthy. Most animals get their nutrients from the food they eat. Most plants get their nutrients from the soil, through their roots.

Sedimentary rock
Sedimentary rock is made up of layers of material that have settled out from water, or sometimes from the air, and over many years have become pressed together into solid rock.

Tide
The tide is the rise and fall of the level of the sea. In most places on the coast you can see this happening twice every day.

Vapour
When water goes into the air in the form of a gas, this is often called water vapour. If the water is boiling, it is called steam.

Volcano
A volcano is an opening in the Earth's crust through which lumps of rock, melted rock, ashes, dust and hot gas are thrown up from deep down in the Earth, sometimes very violently. Often the rock and ashes build up to form a mountain, and the mountain itself may be known as a volcano.